Holi

words & pictures

Text by Sital Gorasia Chapman

First published in 2026 by words & pictures,
an imprint of The Quarto Group.
100 Cummings Center, Suite 265D
Beverly, MA 01915, USA.
T (978) 282-9590 F (978) 283-2742
www.quarto.com

EEA Representation, WTS Tax d.o.o., Žanova ulica 3, 4000 Kranj, Slovenia
www.wts-tax.si

Editor: Anna Brett
Senior Editor: Molly Mead
Designer: Karen Hood
Senior Designer: Mike Henson
Creative Director: Malena Stojić
Associate Publisher: Holly Willsher
Senior Production Controller: Nikki Ingram

ISBN: 978-1-83600-805-7
9 8 7 6 5 4 3 2 1

Manufactured in Guangdong, China TT102025

Holi

Sital Gorasia Chapman

illustrated by Pranami Bora

Happy Holi!

My name is Basanti and this is my twin sister, Anika. I'm super excited because we are getting ready to celebrate my favorite festival, Holi!

Holi is a Hindu celebration
known as the festival of colors
and it marks the beginning of spring.
Celebrations last a whole day,
plus the evening before. This festival
feels extra special to me because
my name, Basanti,
means spring!

Before Holi begins, Anika and I pick flowers from Nani's garden to make gulal, a colored powder that we throw on each other during the festival. It's so much fun!

Nani loves gardening and her garden is always full of color. We collect red roses, purple hibiscus, yellow marigolds, and my favorite, pink jasmine. It looks and smells so lovely!

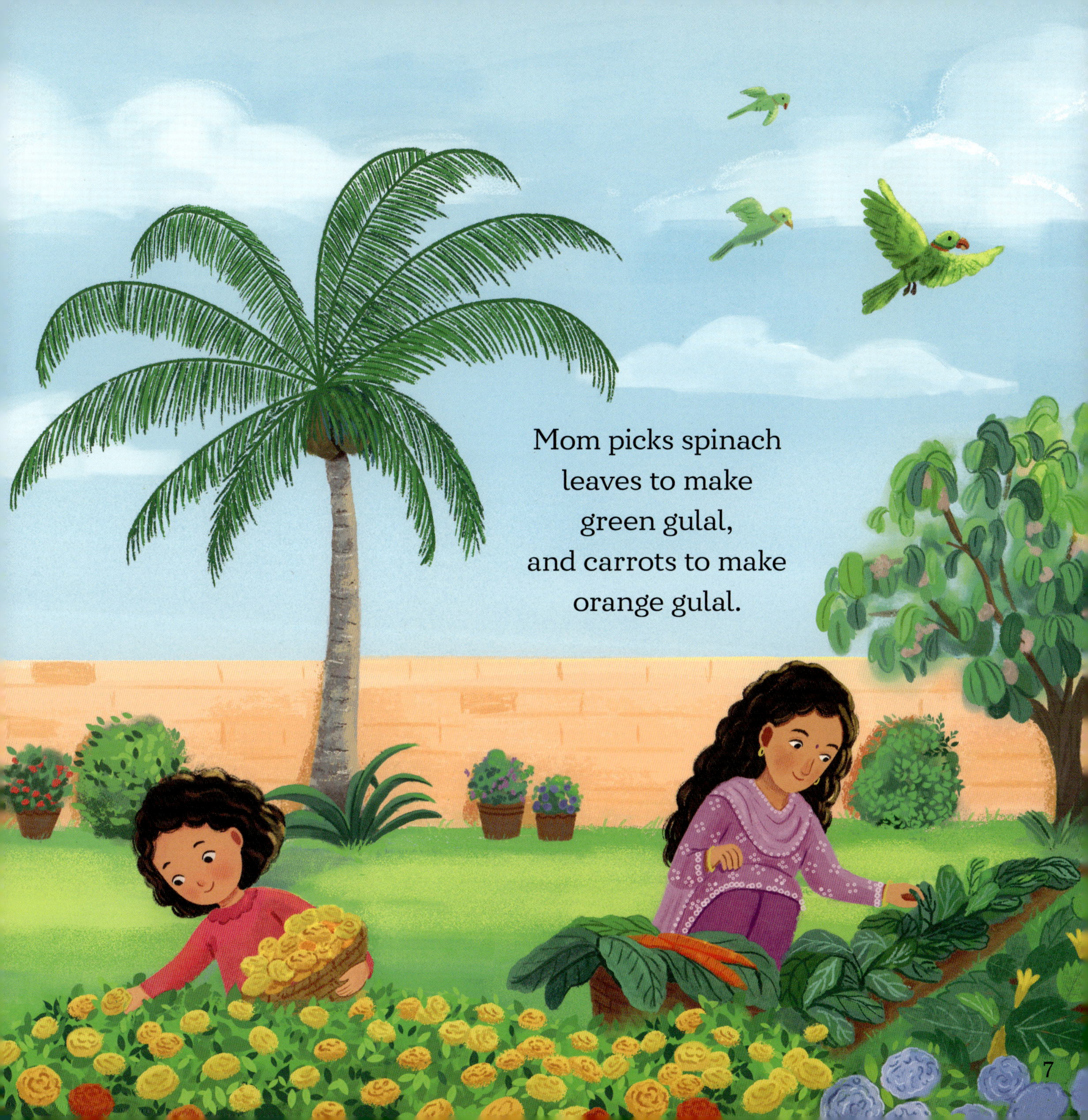

Mom picks spinach leaves to make green gulal, and carrots to make orange gulal.

We pluck off the flower petals and drop them in water. Then Nani boils them to bring out their bright, vibrant colors. Mom juices the carrots and spinach.

Once the bright liquids are cool, we add them to cornstarch to make the colored gulal powders. They look so pretty! We throw gulal during Holi to celebrate love and friendship.

Everything is ready for the Holi festival tomorrow. But tonight is Holika Dahan, or "Little Holi."

Holika Dahan is celebrated on the night of the full moon to honor new beginnings and the victory of good over evil.

We dress in our best clothes and run over to the local park where the festival is taking place this year. All our friends and neighbors are here!

Delicious smells waft over
from the food stalls dotted
around the edge of the field.
Anika and I eat deep-fried
pakoras and spicy samosas—
they are super tasty!

A pile of wood is stacked up to form a bonfire in the center of the field. We stand well back as it is lit. The warm red glow starts in the middle and spreads outward until the whole pile is alight.

We watch the flames dancing in the darkness. Little flecks of orange break away and float off into the night sky like glitter.

We carry coconuts over to the bonfire and then Mom tosses them into the flames. The hard coconut shells represent protection and the white coconut flesh represents inner purity.

We sit around the fire as my Nana tells us the legend of Holika.

"Many moons ago, an evil demon king tormented his people.

He wanted everyone to worship him and would not allow them to practice any religions. He was a bully and everyone was afraid of him.

Only his son, Prahlad, was brave enough to stand up to him. The evil king was furious and decided to get rid of his son."

“The king asked his demon sister, Holika, for help. Holika thought she could trick Prahlad into burning himself on a bonfire. She showed him how her power meant the flames could do no harm.

Prahlad was a good person and worshipped the god Vishnu.

He believed he was protected by Vishnu and would come to no harm whether Holika was being truthful or not.

Prahlad was right—he was saved and good overcame evil as Holika's power failed her and she was destroyed in the flames instead."

We head home to bed after a lovely evening together.

The next morning, I shake Anika
awake extra early. Today is Holi!
I can't wait to celebrate.

We help Mom and Dad prepare some special Holi food. Ghughra is a delicious treat with a sweet center. Mom kneads the dough while Dad mixes semolina with crushed dates and coconut for the filling.

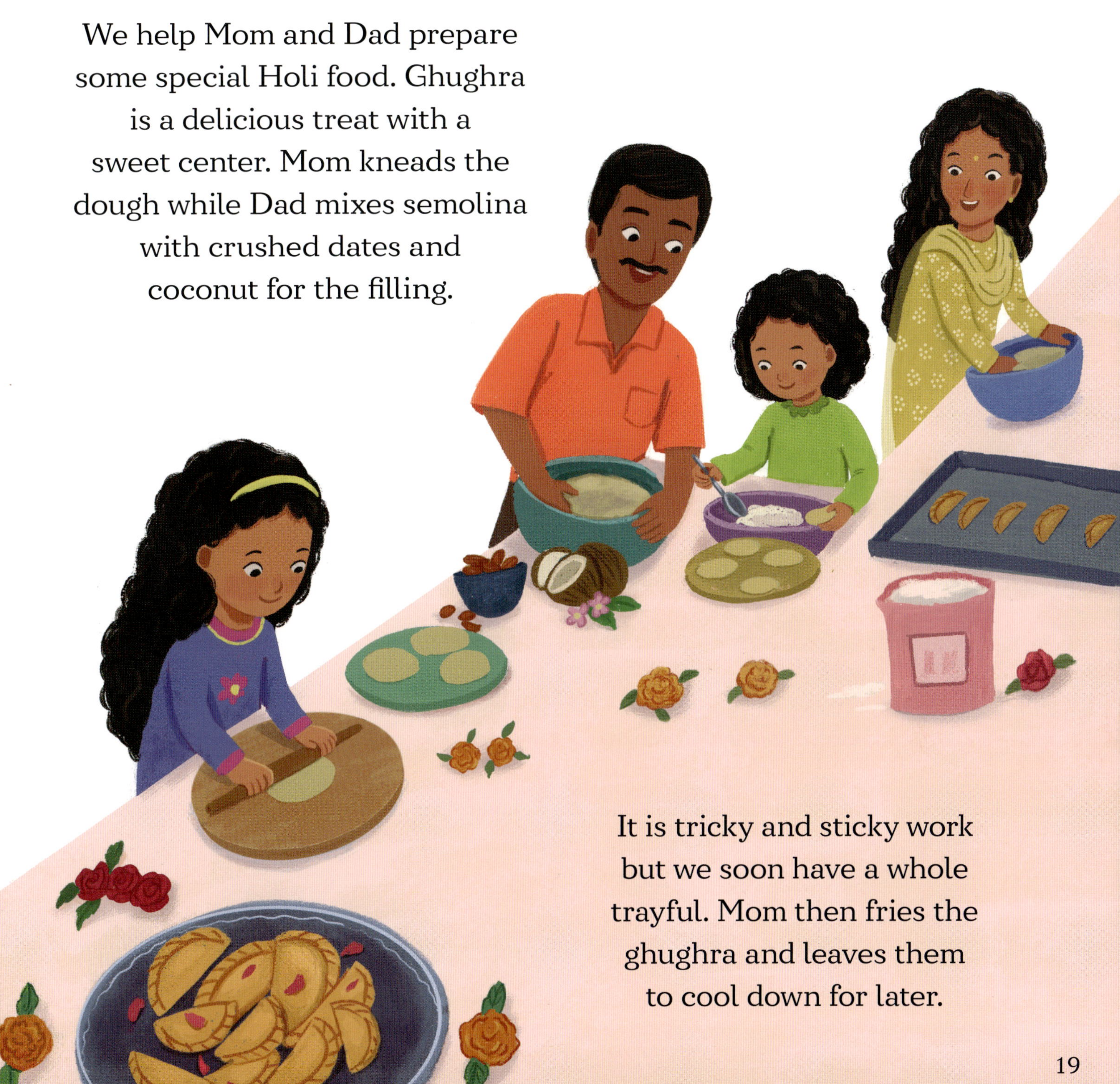

It is tricky and sticky work but we soon have a whole trayful. Mom then fries the ghughra and leaves them to cool down for later.

Finally, it is time for the main event of the Holi festival! We head into the center of town.

We dress in old clothes that we don't mind getting messy. They are mainly white as this will show off the gulal colors better.

There are lots of people here. I wave to some friends from school. Even though Holi is a Hindu festival, it is open to everyone. People of all faiths, ethnicities, and backgrounds are welcome.

The aim is to have fun together.

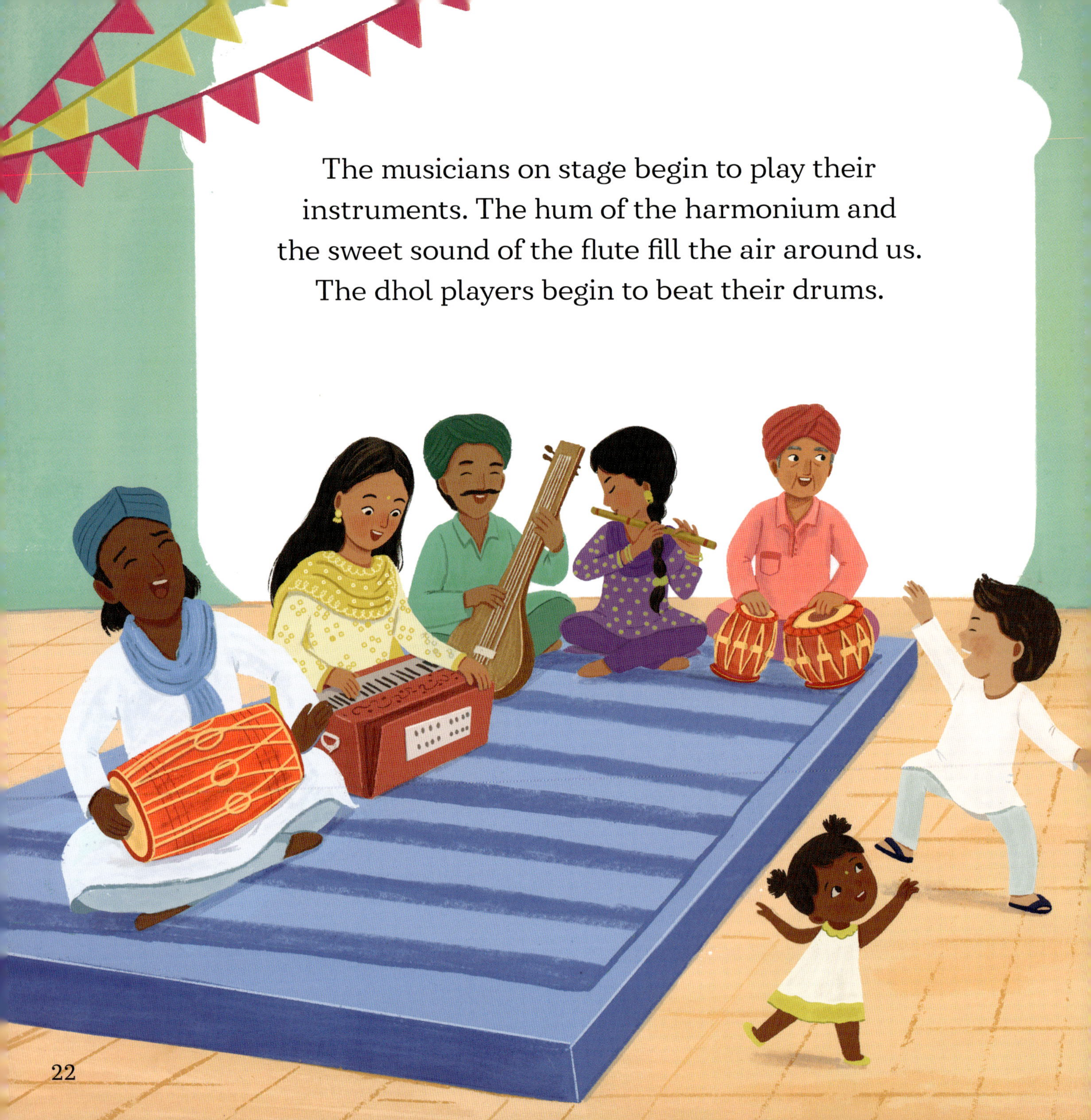

The musicians on stage begin to play their instruments. The hum of the harmonium and the sweet sound of the flute fill the air around us. The dhol players begin to beat their drums.

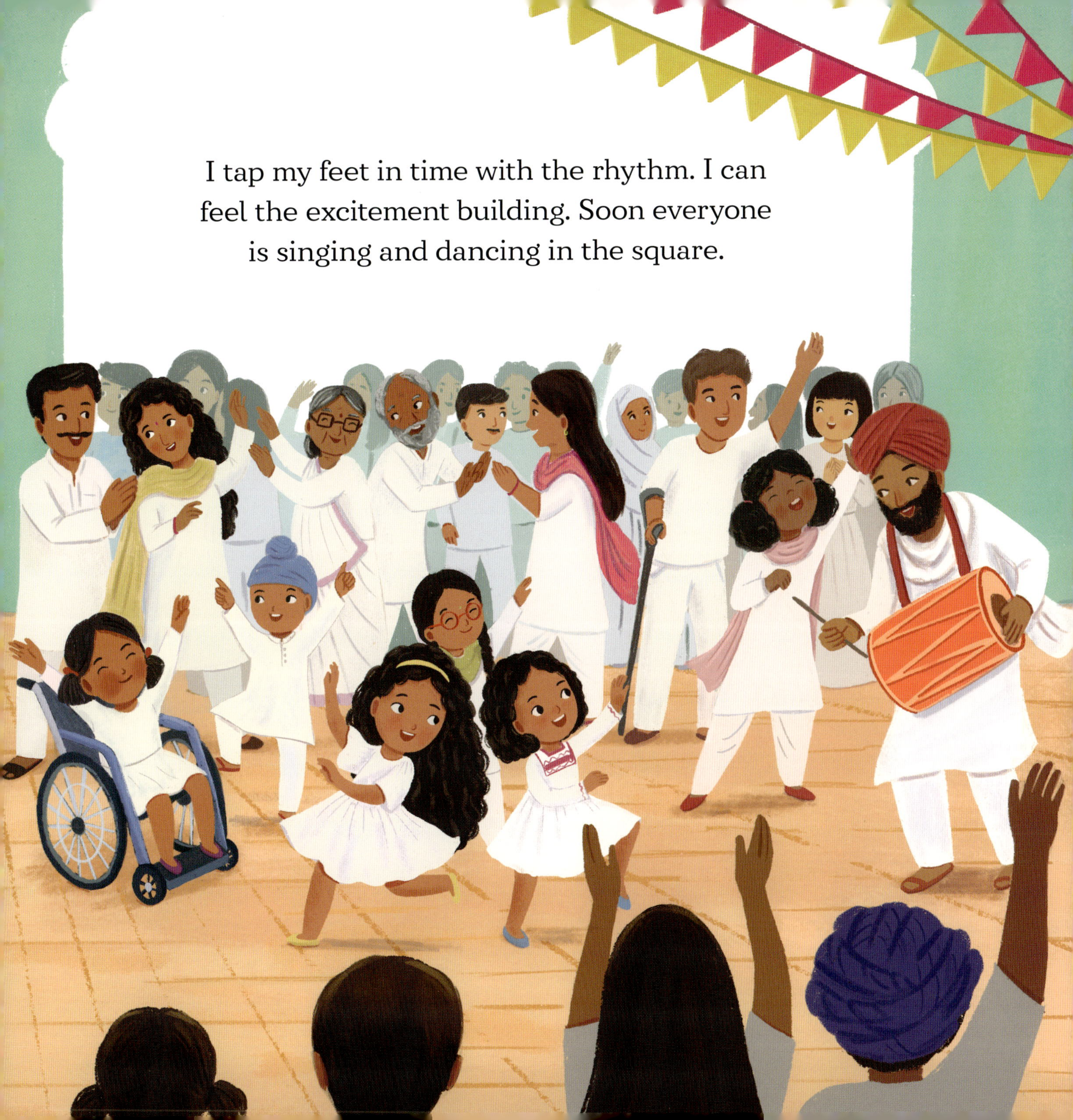

I tap my feet in time with the rhythm. I can feel the excitement building. Soon everyone is singing and dancing in the square.

The first gulal color is thrown. A sprinkling of pink lands on Nana's nose, making him sneeze.

His tray of colored powders is blown into the air like a rainbow cloud.

Mom's sister, Lina Masi, rubs a purple paste on to her cheek and quickly runs away. Mom chases after her and showers her in green and yellow gulal. They both giggle. It's so nice to see the grown-ups playing!

My cousin Arun squirts me with a pichkari—it contains gulal mixed with water. I duck and a jet of blue liquid soaks Nani's white sari.

Nani laughs and, armed with her own pichkaris, squirts colorful water right back at Arun. He is drenched!

I team up with Anika to shower Dad in every shade of gulal we have.

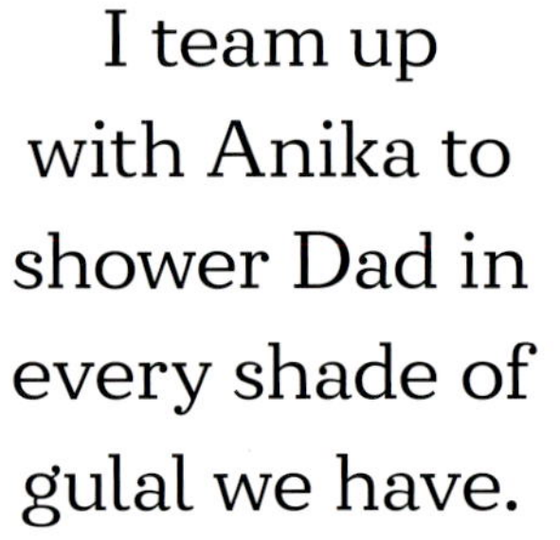

He draws us into a massive colorful cuddle and rubs gulal into our curly brown hair.

Everywhere around us, people are laughing and having fun, enjoying their colorful games. Our white clothes have become a kaleidoscope of bright shades.

Everyone looks colorful and carefree together.

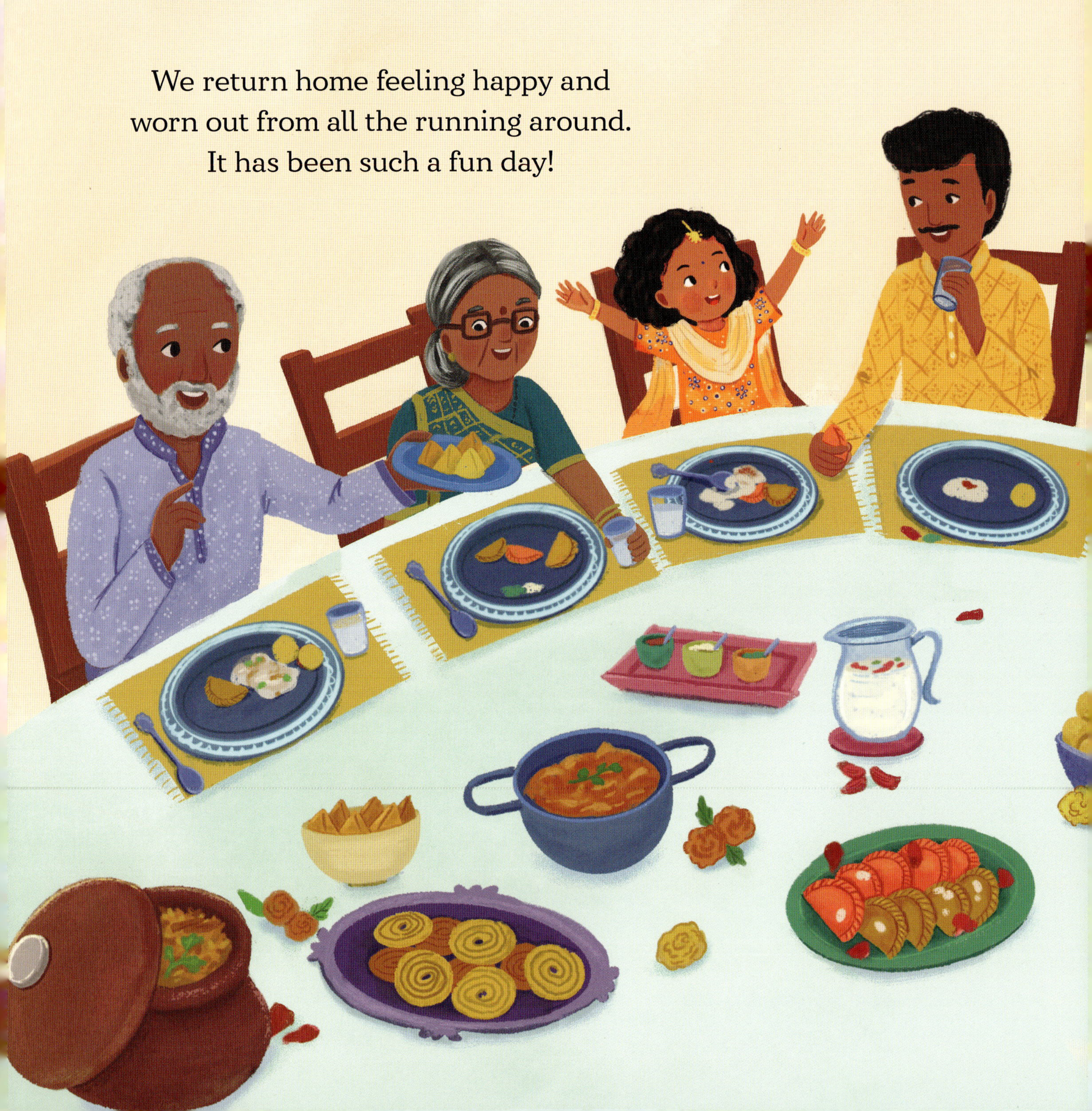

We return home feeling happy and worn out from all the running around. It has been such a fun day!

After we clean ourselves up and change our clothes, it is time for dinner. Lina Masi and Arun join us and bring some tasty snacks with them. We finish our meal with the sweet ghughra we made this morning. Yum!

Holi has been amazing.
I loved making and throwing the
colorful gulal and eating delicious
treats, as well as watching the bonfire
and listening to Nana tell the
story of Holika last night.

Most of all I adored celebrating with the people I love. I feel so lucky that we get to enjoy this festival all over again next year!

Festival of Colors

Holi is a colorful festival celebrated by Hindus and their friends all around the world. It marks the end of the cold, dark winter and welcomes the beginning of spring and new life.

MARCH
FEBRUARY

Holi is celebrated in the Hindu month of Fagan (or Falgun), which usually falls around February or March. The exact date is determined by the full moon.

HINDU CALENDAR

The Hindu calendar follows the lunar cycle rather than a solar cycle to measure time. A solar cycle is the time it takes the Earth to orbit the Sun and is the most common way to measure a year. Months are usually 30 or 31 days in length. A lunar cycle is the time it takes for the moon to pass through all its phases, meaning a lunar month is 29.5 days.

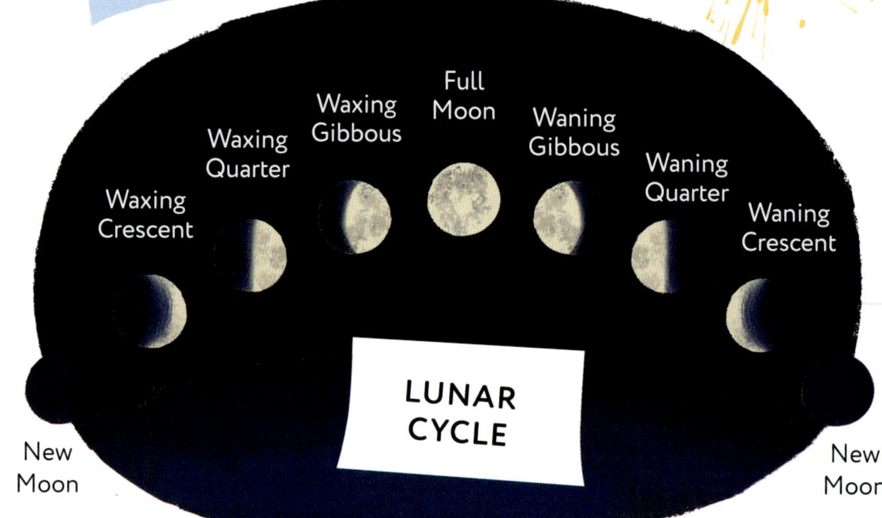

Meet the Gods and Goddesses

There are many gods and goddesses celebrated in Hinduism. Here are a few who are important during Holi.

BRAHMA

The god of creation. He granted Hiranyakashipu (the evil king in the story on pages 14-17) the power of invincibility, which helped him temporarily take over the world.

VISHNU

The god of preservation. He was worshipped by Prahlad, and protected him from Holika's fire. Read more about this story on pages 14–17.

SHIVA

The god of destruction and Parvati's husband. Read more about Shiva on pages 40-41.

PARVATI

The goddess of power and Shiva's wife.

KRISHNA

The god of compassion. His love for Radha is celebrated during Holi. Read their story on pages 36-37.

RADHA

The beloved of Krishna. Associated with love and devotion.

KAMA

The god of love who shot an arrow at Shiva. Rati's husband.

RATI

The goddess of love and Kama's wife.

The Story Behind The Color!

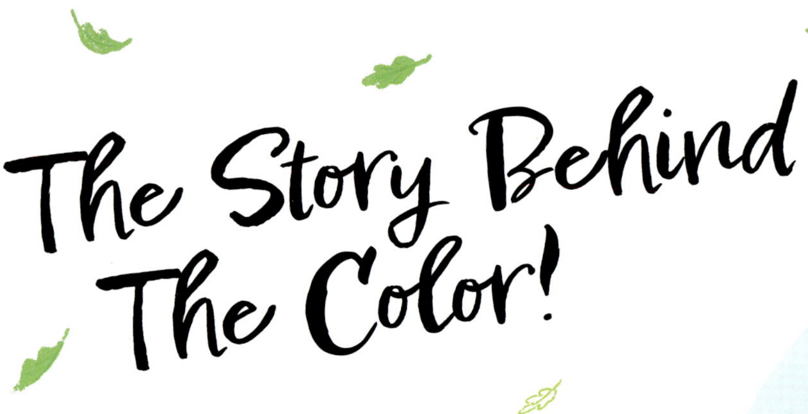

There are many Holi stories in Hindu mythology. One of them is the story of Radha and Krishna, which is thought to be the origin of the color throwing that takes place during Holi.

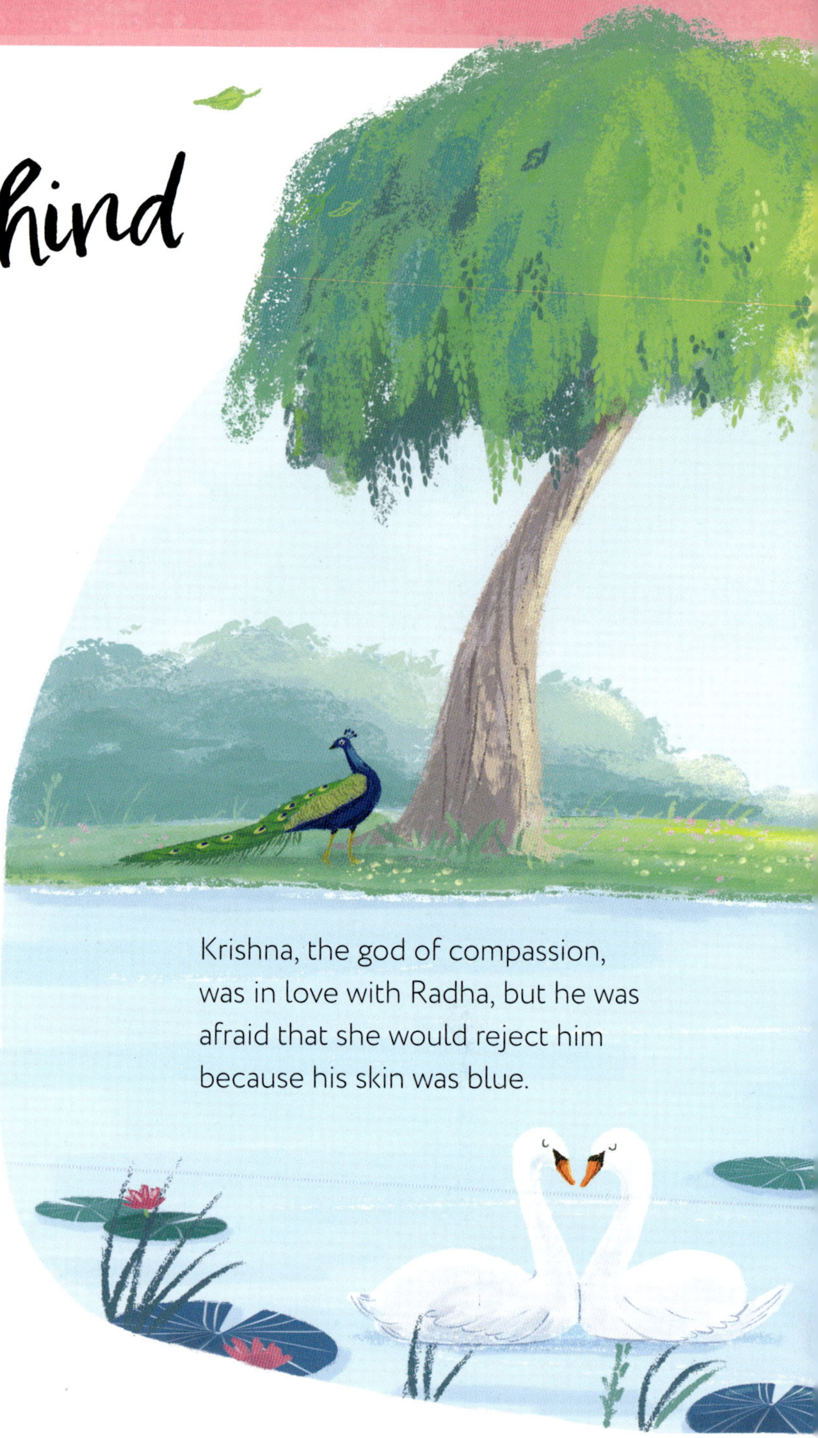

Krishna, the god of compassion, was in love with Radha, but he was afraid that she would reject him because his skin was blue.

His mother didn't think this was true but jokingly suggested that he smear some colors on Radha's face to change it. Krishna was feeling playful so he went ahead!

But Krishna need not have worried, Radha loved him for who he was—each and every part. The color throwing games during Holi celebrate their unconditional love.

Holi Paper Chains

Splashing colored water and powders on friends and family is a fun part of Holi. Why not try doing it with paper?

YOU WILL NEED:

- White printer paper
- Scissors
- Pencil or crayon
- Colorful paints and water
- Paint pots or a plastic plate
- Old newspapers
- Paintbrushes
- A drinking straw
- A grown-up to help

INSTRUCTIONS

1. Make sure to protect your clothes and the area around you so you don't accidentally splash paint anywhere you don't want to! Or you could try doing the activity outside.

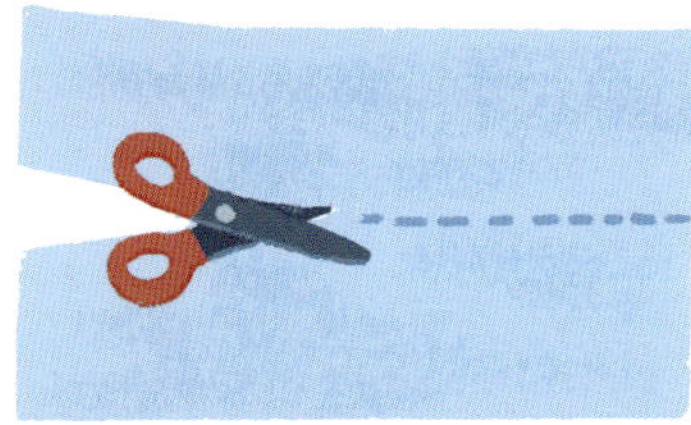

2. Fold a piece of white printer paper in half, lengthways, then open it back up and cut along the crease line to form two long strips.

3. Fold one of the strips in half, then in half again, to make a little booklet.

4. Keeping the booklet closed, draw the outline of a person on the front. Make sure the arms stretch across the entire width of the paper.

5. Cut out the person shape through all the layers of paper, but be sure not to cut off the hands! This way there is still one folded edge of paper left intact. When you unfold the paper, a chain of people will appear.

6. Repeat steps 3-5 with the other strip to make more paper chain friends.

7. Using a variety of pots, or a large plastic plate, mix a range of paint colors separately with a little water to make them all a bit runnier.

8. If indoors, lay out lots of old newspaper and put your cut-out people on top. Dip a paintbrush into your first color and then drip and flick it at the cut-out people.

9. Repeat using different colors until all the cut-out people are splattered with paint.

10. Try blowing through a straw at the cut-out people to see if you can blend some of the different colors together.

11. When you're finished, leave your paper chains to dry.

12. With help from a grown-up, stick the paper chains up. Now sit back and enjoy your cheerful Holi decorations that celebrate friendship and fun!

Shiva and Rati's story

We have already heard two of the stories associated with Holi. But in some parts of India, particularly in the south, there is another story and another reason to celebrate.

According to myth, Shiva (the god of destruction) was in deep meditation and nobody could get his attention, including Parvati (who would later become his wife).

Frustrated, Parvati turned to the god of love, Kama. To try and make Shiva fall in love with Parvati, Kama shot him with a flower of love. But Shiva was angry at being disturbed and used the power of his third eye to burn Kama to a crisp!

Kama's wife, Rati, was rightly very upset and pleaded with Shiva to return her husband. She then performed a 40-day meditation to show her devotion to him. Shiva was impressed and granted her wish to bring Kama back. Love and forgiveness triumphed for both couples and this is what is celebrated at Holi.

Tie-dye a Holi T-shirt

People usually wear white clothes for the Holi festivities, but they don't stay white for long! Create a brightly colored tie-dyed t-shirt that looks like it's come straight out of a gulal shower.

YOU WILL NEED:

- A white cotton t-shirt your grown-up says you can use!
- Water
- Rubber bands
- Tray and bucket
- Fabric or acrylic paint mixed with water so it can be easily poured into a bottle
- Clean spray bottles
- A grown-up to help

INSTRUCTIONS

1. Soak your t-shirt in water and then wring out any excess water, leaving it damp.

DIFFERENT FOLDING STYLES

Crumple

Twist

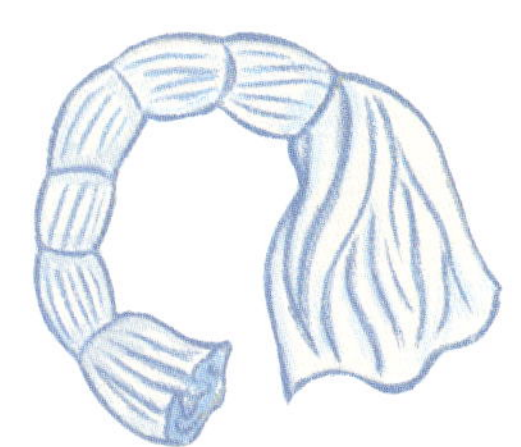

Tie

2. Twist or fold the t-shirt any way you like and secure with some rubber bands. Different folds and twists will make different patterns.

3. Place the t-shirt in the tray or bucket.

4. Pour the watered-down paint into spray bottles and then spray your t-shirt. Using two or three different colors will look good.

5. Let the t-shirt dry for around three hours before removing the rubber bands.

6. Unfold the t-shirt and let it dry completely to set the paint.

7. It's then best to put your t-shirt in the washing machine (on its own!) before wearing it, just in case the colors transfer or run.

Red is my favorite color!

Colorful Kulfi

Kulfi is a traditional Indian frozen dessert. This is an easy recipe with no cooking or churning required. Try different flavors to make a treat that celebrates the colors of Holi!

YOU WILL NEED:

- A ripe mango, a handful of strawberries, a small bowl of blueberries, or any other colorful fruit
- 1 ¼ cup heavy cream (or plant-based alternative)
- 1 ⅔ cup sweetened condensed milk (or plant-based alternative)
- ½ teaspoon ground cardamom
- Kitchen utensils
- A grown-up to help

TIP: Freeze the blueberries first to make their color much brighter!

INSTRUCTIONS

1. Wash all the fruit, then ask a grown-up to help you peel and slice the mango and hull the strawberries.

2. Mash each fruit through a sieve into its own bowl to remove any seeds or fibers. You should be left with smooth purées in different colors.

3. Whip the heavy cream in a large bowl with a whisk. It takes a while and a bit of effort but it should form soft peaks.

4. Pour the sweetened condensed milk into a separate bowl and add a spoonful of the whipped cream.

5. Mix thoroughly and then pour the whole mixture into the whipped cream.

6. Add in the cardamom then gently fold it all together with a spatula until silky smooth.

7. Divide the cream mixture into the bowls containing the fruit purées and give each of them a good stir.

8. Pour the mixtures into airtight tubs and freeze for 6 to 8 hours until the dessert is set.

9. Remove from the freezer a few minutes before serving and scoop into bowls.

Enjoy your cool, colorful treat!

Quiz

The color blue represents the gods.

Try this quiz to see how much you can remember about Holi.

1. What is Holi known as?

a. The festival of gold

b. The festival of shadows

c. The festival of colors

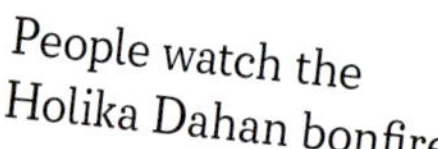

People watch the Holika Dahan bonfire

2. What was the name of Prahlad's demon aunt?

a. Holika

b. Holisha

c. Monica

3. Holi marks the beginning of which season?

a. Summer

b. Spring

c. Winter

4. How long is Holi celebrated for?

a. A night and a day

b. One week

c. One day

5. What do people throw during Holi?

a. Colored powder

b. Rice

c. Confetti

6. When is Holika Dahan celebrated?

a. The night of the new moon

b. The night of the full moon

c. After breakfast

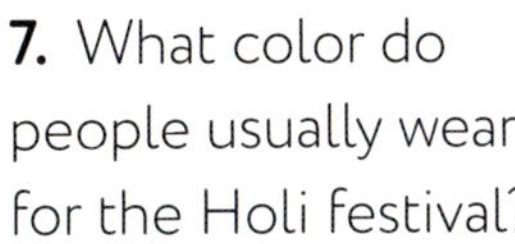

Holi can get very messy!

7. What color do people usually wear for the Holi festival?

a. White

b. Blue

c. Green

8. What is a dhol?

a. A trumpet

b. A drum

c. A flute

9. Why is color thrown during Holi?

a. To celebrate school

b. To celebrate love and friendship

c. To ward off bad luck

10. Who is Shiva?

a. The god of creation

b. The god of love

c. The god of destruction

Answers on the next page!

Answers

1. c. The festival of colors
2. a. Holika
3. b. Spring
4. a. A night and a day
5. a. Colored powder
6. b. The night of the full moon
7. a. White
8. b. A drum
9. b. To celebrate love and friendship
10. c. The god of destruction

IMAGE CREDITS P34 top right: David Woods / Dreamstime. P46 bottom left: C.Slawik / Juniors, Juniors Bildarchiv GmbH / Alamy. P47 center left: Tim Gainey / Alamy. P47 top right: Mark MacEwen / Nature Picture Library / Alamy.